THE VALUES LIBRARY
DETERMINATION

Florence Griffith Joyner of California raises her arms in victory as she wins the women's 100 meters final at the Seoul Olympics.

THE VALUES LIBRARY

DETERMINATION

Eleanor Ayer

THE ROSEN PUBLISHING GROUP, INC.
NEW YORK

Published in 1991 by The Rosen Publishing Group, Inc.
29 East 21st Street, New York, NY 10010.

First Edition
Copyright © 1991 by The Rosen Publishing Group, Inc.

All rights reserved. No part of this book may be reproduced in any form without permission, in writing, from the publisher, except by a reviewer.

Printed in Canada

Library of Congress Cataloging-in-Publication Data

Ayer, Eleanor H.
    Determination / Eleanor H. Ayer. — 1st ed.
    (The Values library)
    Includes bibliographical references and index.
    Summary: Examines the meaning and value of determination and how it can be developed, used in combination with persistence, and maintained in the face of obstacles.
    ISBN 0-8239-1226-4
    1. Determination (Personality trait)—juvenile literature. 2. Persistence—juvenile literature. 3. Determination (Personality trait)—Case studies—juvenile literature. [1. Determination (Personality trait) 2. Persistence.] I. Title. II. Series.
BF698.35.D48A94   1991
155.2'32—dc20   91-6406
                                                              CIP
                                                                AC

CONTENTS

Chapter One	WHAT IS DETERMINATION?	7
Chapter Two	HURDLES AND OBSTACLES	15
Chapter Three	DETERMINATION: WHEN AND WHY DO YOU NEED IT?	27
Chapter Four	HOW *YOU* CAN BECOME A DETERMINED PERSON	35
Chapter Five	WHAT IF YOU FAIL?	43
Chapter Six	THE IMPORTANCE OF BEING POSITIVE	53
Glossary: Explaining New Words		59
For Further Reading		61
Index		63

Perfecting skills takes many hours of practice and a will to keep on trying.

1

WHAT IS DETERMINATION?

IF AT FIRST YOU DON'T SUCCEED, TRY, TRY AGAIN. It's easy to say. But when you have one failure after another, it's hard to try again. You think, "I don't want to do this any more. I'm tired of failing. I want to quit." Then your inner voice says, "But you want to reach your goal, don't you?" Of course you do, so you try again. By trying again you show *determination*.

Set a Goal

The first step in showing determination is setting your goal. You decide what you want to do. The second step is working hard to reach that goal, no matter what problems may come along.

Without determination, Blanca Rodriguez-Ybarra might still be picking weeds in a Colorado bean field. Blanca's family were migrant workers. Each year in May they left home in south Texas to work in the fields up north.

Chapter One

"My mother only finished first grade. My father got through third," says Blanca. "But they knew education was important. They wanted us to learn." It wasn't easy.

"Nothing in school made sense because we didn't speak English. We were punished for speaking Spanish. At lunch, I would hide my tortilla. I didn't want kids to know we were too poor to buy a 25-cent loaf of bread."

The year Blanca was 13 she set her big goal—to get out of the fields. She got a job in a meat plant. But her determination didn't stop there. She graduated from high school. Soon she was married with two small children. But she started college. By the time she finished, she had a third baby!

Today Blanca has a master's degree—the next step after college. She is working on a second master's. Without determination she never would have reached these goals. "I've always been a survivor," Blanca says. "I'll do whatever I have to do to keep going."

Decide firmly to reach a goal. The easy part is deciding. The hard part is doing. You need to have *faith* that you can and will reach your goal. Determination takes *patience* and *persistence,* and the will to try, try again. Determination takes *courage.* If you are a determined person you are not afraid to fail. You are not afraid to stand up for your *beliefs*.

What Is Determination?

Baik Sun-Hak was a Korean War orphan when he was 12 years old. He lived in rags and ate out of garbage cans. But he was determined to live better. He got a job washing clothes and cleaning toilets for American soldiers. His pay was food. Two years later Baik went to the city of Seoul. He worked as a janitor in a factory that made boys' hats. Some days he worked 18 hours.

Persistence—the strength to keep going even when you feel like quitting—is a big part of determination. In just four years Baik was the manager of two hat stores and a factory. At 19 he quit to start his own hat business. He rented a small shop. All day he sold hats. When his shop closed, he worked until early morning making more hats to sell the next day.

Baik's determination paid off. Today he has 3,800 people in five countries working for him. His companies make more than half of all the baseball caps sold in America. Baik is a very rich man.

Determination can mean believing in something when very few others do. In Christopher Columbus's day, people in Europe liked to buy spices and silks from India and China. But it was a long trip by land. Columbus was determined to find a shorter route.

Only a few people then believed that the world was round. Columbus was one of them When he said he was

Chapter One

Preston Tucker (right) pursued his dream to build the world's finest car, even though many people said it was impossible. Here, Tucker's daughter christens one of the few completed cars.

---

going to travel *west* from Spain to reach India, people thought he was crazy. The king of Portugal would not help. The queen of Spain also said no.

But Columbus did not give up. He believed he was right. Finally, the queen of Spain agreed, and Columbus set sail in 1492. He never reached India, but instead discovered the New World. If he had not been determined, Columbus's name would be lost in history.

Determination sometimes requires courage. Preston Tucker thought he could build the finest car ever built. His would be the first car with the engine in the back. The front fenders and headlights would turn with the wheels to light the road better at night. His car would get up to 35 miles per gallon—unheard of in 1947!

Tucker sold stock in his new company to raise money to build the cars. But the government did not believe Tucker could build such a car. California and Michigan would not even let him sell stock.

Still, Preston Tucker had courage. In spite of a big lawsuit, he built 50 cars. They were beautiful! The world Inventors Exposition called his car "the best invention of the year."

Fifty cars were all that the Tucker Corporation ever made. But most of those are still running. A movie was made about Tucker. The theme of the movie was determination—something Preston Tucker knew a lot about.

11
What Is Determination?

Chapter One

Nearly every major step in history has taken determination. People have made a *commitment.* They have pledged to work toward a goal.

During the 1970s, Lech Walesa worked in the shipyards at Gdansk, Poland. The hours were long, and the pay was very low. Even when he was paid, there was little to buy in the stores. The communist government ruled the Polish people in a harsh way. Determined to change that, Walesa joined with other workers to start the Solidarity Movement.

Solidarity wanted workers to be able to make the rules under which they would work. They did not want the communist government to have strict control over their jobs. But the communists would not give the workers this freedom. The leaders of Solidarity were harassed and thrown in jail.

All through the 1980s, Walesa kept his commitment, despite the danger. Finally, in 1989, that determination paid off. The communists agreed to make Solidarity legal. Solidarity leaders won the next election. The communists no longer rule Poland. This big step forward in history is thanks to the determination of Lech Walesa and others like him.

When have *you* needed determination? Maybe you weren't chosen for a sports team. What did you do? Did

13
What Is Determination?

you grumble that the coach was unfair? Did you curse your bad luck? Or did you show determination? If you did, you got out there and practiced—even though you weren't playing on the team. If you had faith in yourself you said, "I *know* I can make it next year." And with that kind of determination, you probably did.

Helen Keller (left) overcame being blind, deaf and mute with great determination and help from her teacher Anne Sullivan.

2

HURDLES AND OBSTACLES

GO TO A QUIET ROOM. CLOSE YOUR EYES. Stick your fingers in your ears. Do not speak. You are now hearing and seeing all that Helen Keller ever saw or heard in her life. Only after many years could she speak. Even then she was very hard to understand.

What if you had to live the rest of your life this way? Do you think you'd graduate with high honors from one of the best colleges in the country? Would you tour the world giving speeches? Would the president of the United States give you the highest award a citizen can get? Perhaps so, if you have as much determination as Helen Keller had.

Helen became blind, deaf, and mute after an illness she had when she was a baby. Her parents hired a special teacher for her, Anne Sullivan. Anne used a doll to teach Helen the Braille alphabet. Braille is a system of

Chapter Two

raised dots that blind people can learn to read by feeling. Anne held Helen's hand palm-up and pressed into it the Braille symbols for d-o-l-l. This is how Helen learned to read. She learned to talk by holding her hand on Anne's throat. She could feel the vibrations of Anne's voice as she spoke.

Helen Keller was determined to live a useful life. Because of her disabilities, she had to work much harder than most people. But she showed *self-discipline*. She would not let herself quit, even though learning how to speak and read was very hard.

Anne Sullivan showed great determination, too. She was patient. She did not get discouraged working with someone who could not see, hear, or speak to her.

Meeting the Obstacles in Our Lives

If we let them, obstacles will keep us from reaching our goals. Determination helps us overcome obstacles. The obstacles in Helen Keller's life were physical. They affected her body. Sometimes the obstacles are put there by society.

More than anything else, Florence Sabin wanted to be a doctor. But in the late 1800s, very few girls even went to high school. Society said it was wrong for a woman to work away from home. A woman's job was to be a good wife and mother. But Florence Sabin didn't want to

17
Hurdles and Obstacles

Learning to overcome disabilities takes effort and determination.

marry. She wanted to study. Her sister thought she should be a teacher because there would not be so many obstacles. But Florence was determined to become a doctor.

In 1923, Dr. Florence Sabin was named one of the world's 12 greatest women. She had been persistent. "You can become whatever you want to become," Sabin believed. She stuck to her dream. And it paid off.

Race or Religion Can Be an Obstacle

Sometimes there are obstacles put in a person's life because of his or her race or religion. American Indians were sent to live on reservations. Black Americans were not allowed to vote or get certain jobs. In Germany in the 1930s and 1940s, Jews lost all their human rights. Germany's leader, Adolf Hitler, hated Jews. His plan was to kill them all.

As part of his plan, Hitler built concentration camps. His men rounded up all the Jews they could find and shipped them in cattle cars to the camps. Here they were beaten, tortured, starved and murdered. They were made to work terribly hard.

Millions of Jews died in the camps. Many who did not die showed a great determination to live. Helen Waterford was one of those. Helen and her husband were shipped to a camp in Poland where millions of Jews were killed with a deadly gas. Helen's husband was killed. She was sent to a women's work camp. Each woman only had one dress. Many had no shoes. None had coats, although the winters were long and cold. Dinner was a thin soup in which potatoes or turnips had been cooked and taken out. Four women drank from one bowl. They had no spoons.

"So many women lost hope. The cold weather, so little food, and great weakness made them want to die. When they started feeling this way, it was no more than two days before they were dead."

What helped Helen Waterford live? "Very early I learned what it takes to be a strong person. When I was as close to death as anyone can come, I depended on myself. That was my faith."

Society put a terrible obstacle in Helen Waterford's life. But she was determined to live. Her great faith in herself helped her overcome that obstacle.

Maybe Your Goal Is the Obstacle

Sometimes the obstacle is your goal itself. What you want to do may be so hard that it seems impossible. Louis Pasteur was a French scientist in the 1800s. Scientists then did not know what caused diseases. Pasteur believed that diseases were caused by bacteria. He was determined to prove he was right.

Determination means trying again if your first attempts do not succeed.

Hurdles and Obstacles

Pasteur worked long hours in his lab. He read and studied. He did many experiments. His ideas were very hard to prove. Many scientists did not agree with him. But Pasteur believed in himself.

Louis Pasteur had a very tough goal. Luckily for the world, he had faith in himself. He found a cure for rabies. He discovered that pasteurizing milk would stop germs from growing in it. Louis Pasteur was one of the world's greatest scientists. Would he have been so great if he had not been so determined? It's easy to give up when people say you are wrong. A tough goal is a big obstacle to overcome.

Exploring the Grand Canyon was also a tough goal. A non-Indian person had never done it when John Wesley Powell tried in 1869. There were no maps. Powell's men would draw the first maps. There were no photographs. Powell's men would take those, too.

The first trip left Green River, Wyoming, on May 24. Ten men set out in four boats. Powell had only one arm. He had lost the other fighting in the Civil War. The rapids (fast, rough water) at some places in the river were worse than Powell had imagined. The group ran short of supplies. Three men quit along the way.

Two boats and a lot of the information gathered by the group were lost during the trip. Powell, six men, and two boats came out of the Grand Canyon in Nevada on

Chapter Two

August 30. Powell had accomplished a lot, but he was not satisfied. He was determined to try again.

During the 1870s, John Wesley Powell went back to explore more of the Grand Canyon. He could have quit after the first trip, which had made him a hero. But Powell knew he could do better.

His goal was difficult. The Grand Canyon is a huge, wild area. But he was determined to explore all of the canyon. Because of his determination, Powell is called the Father of the Grand Canyon.

Obstacles Can Take You by Surprise

You may start out being very sure you can reach your goal. Things go well. Then the obstacle drops like a bomb. This happened to hundreds of families who came to the United States to start a new life in the early 1900s. The obstacles hit them at Ellis Island. This was the place in New York where all immigrants had to stop before they could enter the country.

The Chekov family—six children and their parents—left Russia in 1905. For two years they had saved to come to the United States. It was a great day when they finally got on the boat. They were leaving a cruel government. They were free!

23
Hurdles and Obstacles

Chinese writing, or calligraphy, is a fine art that demands discipline and patience.

Chapter Two

The trip to America took many days. At Ellis Island they waited for hours and hours to be checked. At last a man with a white chalk came to their group. He looked at each person very carefully. He shined a light in the eyes of Leika, their 16-year-old girl. On her coat he made a big X with the chalk.

Soon the family learned the awful truth. The man said Leika had glaucoma, a disease of the eyes. She could not enter the United States. The Chekovs had two choices. They could all go back to Russia, where they would probably be killed. Or Leika could go back alone to live with an aunt where she might be safe.

A huge obstacle had taken them by surprise. But the Chekovs were determined not to quit. Leika would go back to Russia. The family would work and send money so she could go to a doctor. One day, they hoped, Leika would be well enough to come to the United States again.

What obstacles have you had to overcome in your life?
- Were they physical or mental?
- Were the obstacles put there by society?
- Was your goal so tough that it was an obstacle in itself?
- Did an obstacle take you by surprise just before you reached your goal?
- Did determination help you overcome your obstacles?

Hurdles and Obstacles

Determination is a theme in many books. Western writer Louis L'Amour's heroes are full of determination. In one of his books, *North to the Rails*, a family hires an out-of-work cowboy to trail its herd of cattle north to sell. The family is out of money. Selling the cattle is their last hope.

The cowboy runs into many obstacles. The herd is attacked. There is a terrible storm. The cowboy is shot. He loses the herd. But he does not give up. The cowboy is determined to get the family its money. In the end, because of his determination, he does.

"Nothing that comes easy is worth having." Ever heard this saying? If you set tough goals for yourself, they won't be easy to reach. There will be obstacles along the way. But with determination, you'll get there. And when you do, you'll be very proud of yourself!

Determination is needed when one aims for perfection.

3

DETERMINATION: WHEN AND WHY DO YOU NEED IT?

OUTSIDE THE TINY SHACK AN ARTIC BLIZZARD HOWLED. The men inside were hungry. They were *very* tired. Some were sick. Robert E. Peary, the group's leader, would soon lose his legs completely to frostbite.

Determination Means Taking Risks

It was 1899. Robert Peary, with 6 men and 30 sled dogs, was trying to find the North Pole. No one had ever been there before. For six weeks after his toes were cut off, Peary lay on his cot. He kept saying to himself, "I will find a way or make one." This was Peary's motto.

Fifty-two degrees below zero was as warm as it ever got. Food was running low. It looked as if the men would not reach the North Pole. Indeed, they didn't reach their goal that year. Or the next. Or the next. But they kept coming back.

Nine years after the doctor cut off his toes, Robert Peary left on his fifth trip in search of the pole. On April

Chapter Three

6, 1909, he, another man from his group, and six Eskimo guides reached the North Pole. Peary had not *found* a way. He had *made* one. It had taken great determination and courage.

Peary's goal was very difficult. It was dangerous. He was trying to do what no other person had ever done. But he believed his goal was worth the risks. It's easy for us to look back and say, "Sure, I'd take those risks. Look what a hero he is!" But what if Peary hadn't reached his goal? He probably wouldn't have been a hero. Then would it have been worth the risks?

A person with determination would say "yes." You need to take risks if you hope to reach a tough goal. You need determination to keep moving toward your goal. Without it, it's very easy to give up.

Standing Up for Your Beliefs

Remember the Pilgrims who came to America on the *Mayflower*? The Pilgrims lived in England in the early 1600s. They did not believe in what the Church of England taught, so they decided to form their own church. But the English government would not allow this.

First they fled to Holland, where they could live in peace. But there they saw their children growing up Dutch and speaking Dutch. This made them unhappy. They wanted their children raised in the English way.

Standing up for the things you believe in takes courage and faith in yourself.

Chapter Three

The Pilgrims knew they couldn't go back to England. But they were determined to find a place where they could live the way they wanted. They made a plan to go to the New World, what is now North America.

In September 1620, two ships set sail. One of the ships had trouble and could not go on. All of its 101 passengers crowded onto the *Mayflower.* It was a terrible trip, and many people died. Others were very sick. Still, the Pilgrims were determined to reach their goal. They would not turn back. On November 21, after 66 horrible days on the ocean, their ship reached America. The Pilgrims set up their town at Plymouth, in what is now Massachusetts.

They had little food, and there was much sickness that winter. By April, when the *Mayflower* was ready to go back to England, half the people had died. Did the rest give up and go back with the ship? No. They were determined to stay.

The Pilgrims stood up for their beliefs. But it took a lot of determination. Have you ever had to stand up for your beliefs? Maybe you believe it's wrong to drink beer even though many of your friends drink. It gets harder for you to stay with your crowd. They think you're weird and different. You're not as popular as you used to be. What do you do? Do you give in and start drinking? Or do you stand up for your beliefs?

Determination: When and Why Do You Need It?

It's a tough choice. But you must always do what your inner voice tells you is right. Be honest with yourself. It's often not easy to stand up for your beliefs. You may find yourself alone, like Louis Pasteur.

Is It Good Luck or Hard Work?

"Good luck" is really determination plus hard work. Yolanda Washington was 16 and pregnant. Her friends were sure she'd marry Jessie. Her mother thought so, too. Jessie said he was ready. But Yolanda wasn't. She didn't think a rushed marriage to Jessie was the answer.

"It seemed like everyone was against me. Jessie couldn't believe I'd say 'no.' Mama didn't understand. Daddy said I was crazy. 'Where do you think you'll get the money for this baby? Nobody hires black girls that are pregnant and didn't finish high school.' But I'd made one mistake and I'd made up my mind not to make another. I was determined not to get married."

Today Yolanda's friends say she's been lucky. She has a good job and her own apartment. Was it luck that got Yolanda where she is today? No. It was determination.

Yolanda finished her junior year two weeks before the baby was born. "It was really hard going to school when I was pregnant. I was so tired all the time."

That summer she moved in with her older sister. She worked nights at a fast-food place and her sister stayed

Combining studies with motherhood takes an extra strong desire to reach a goal.

Determination: When and Why Do You Need It?

with the baby. When school started again, she made plans with her teachers to take her work home.

"But it was tough to study with the baby crying and needing something all the time. At night I'd go to work until 1 A.M. I came home and slept three or four hours and got up with the baby again. Somehow I made it. But it's been a lot of hard work."

Determination means hard work. Michael Jordan, the Chicago Bulls basketball star, knows that. "I've always believed I could do anything I wanted. You have to expect things of yourself before you can do them."

Believing is the first part. You need determination and faith in yourself that you *can* reach a goal. The second part is hard work. "When I was a kid," said Jordan, "I practiced so hard I wore out the backyard court." Still, he didn't make the high school team. But he kept practicing and went on to college at the University of North Carolina. His team won the NCAA championship. Today, many people say that Michael Jordan is the best athlete in the United States. What got him there? Determination plus hard work.

Success is mostly hard work. Thomas Edison, the great inventor of the electric light and the phonograph, was a very determined man. It was he who said, "Genius is *1* percent inspiration and 99 percent perspiration."

You can develop skills to further your long-range goals.

4

HOW *YOU* CAN BECOME A DETERMINED PERSON

DETERMINATION—IT'S NOT SOMETHING THAT LUCKY PEOPLE are born with and unlucky people aren't. Anyone can become a determined person. You build determination inside you.

Start with a Goal

What is it you *really* want to do? Be exact. If your goal is not clear you won't know where to start. Perhaps you like computers. You say your goal is to get a job where you can work with computers. But nearly all businesses use computers. You need to be more exact. Do you want a job in a bank where you work with numbers on a computer? Do you want to work for a newspaper setting type on a computer?

Set Up Steps to Reach Your Goal

The bigger your goal, the more steps it will take to reach it. These steps are little goals on the way to your big goal. An old Chinese proverb says, "A trip of a thousand miles begins with a single step."

After you list your steps, put them in order. Now you're ready to begin. "It's important to start," says Wally Amos. Wally started *Famous Amos'* chocolate chip cookies. Today he is one of the most successful businessmen in America.

Start Right from Where You Are

Getting a job at *The New York Times* isn't your first step in working for a newspaper. Begin where you are. Say you're in the 10th grade. Are you taking a computer or typing class now? If not, sign up. That's your first goal. If you're already in a computer class, is there an after-school class or computer club you could join?

Be Proud of Yourself

When you reach that first goal take time to say, "Nice going! I've made a start. I can see that I'm really on my way." But don't stop there. Begin working on the next step. What about joining the school newspaper? If your school doesn't have one, go to the newspaper office nearest you. Tell them you'd like to volunteer (work for free). Start by doing any job you can, even if it's dumping the trash. Work hard. If you show people you are a hard worker and ready to learn, they'll want to help you.

Focus on What You Can Do

Focus on what you can do, not on what you can't do. At 28 years old, W. Mitchell was healthy and well liked. He flew airplanes. He drove a cable car in San Francisco. He also rode motorcycles, until an accident on one nearly killed him. He was burned over 65 percent of his body. He had 13 blood transfusions and 16 operations on his skin. His body looked horrible. But W. Mitchell is not a quitter.

"I am in charge of my own spaceship. I could look at this as a setback or as a starting point. I chose it as a starting point."

After many months of healing, he went back to flying. He and his friends also started one of the most successful wood stove companies in the United States. Then disaster struck again. The plane Mitchell was flying crashed. He was paralyzed. He could no longer use his legs. Still he would not quit.

Today W. Mitchell has a beautiful wife and a lot of money. He makes speeches all over the country. He skydives. He goes river rafting. Yet his body is covered with scars from the burns. Most of his fingers are missing. And he still can't walk.

Many jobs for young people offer a chance to explore special interests while gaining valuable experience for future careers.

How *You* Can Become a Determined Person

"Before all of this happened to me, there were 10,000 things I could do. Now there are 9,000. I could spend the rest of my life dwelling on the 1,000 that I lost. But I choose to focus on the 9,000 that are left."

Find People Who Can Help You Reach Your Goals

At your newspaper job, talk to the people who run the computers. How did they get started? What kind of training did they need? Where did they get it? What advice do they have for you about getting a job working with computers? Let them know you really want to learn. Show them you're interested and ready to work hard. Most people will be very glad to help you.

Be Willing to Do Whatever It Takes to Reach Your Goal

"But I'll have to give up my paying job to work at the newspaper for free," you say. Yes, but think of what you'll be learning. Think of the people you'll meet who can help you toward your goal. You may not have money in your pocket for a while. Maybe you'll have to give up a few things. But isn't your goal worth some sacrifices?

Chapter Four

General Colin Powell overcame discouraging circumstances to become America's highest-ranking military officer.

Reaching Your Goal Is Usually an Uphill Battle

General Colin Powell holds the highest job in the American military. He is head of the Joint Chiefs of Staff. This means he is the president's top military advisor. Powell is the first black man to hold this high position. But it took determination for him to get to the top.

General Powell was born in Harlem. His parents were poor people who had come from Jamaica. They wanted their son's life to be better. "Get a good education," they told him. "Make something of your life." But even with that good advice, Powell says, he still fooled around too much in school. He decided he wanted to go to graduate school after college. Graduate school would help him get a better job in the army. But the officer in charge had bad news. "Your college grades aren't good enough."

Learn from Your Mistakes

Powell knew he had made a mistake by not working harder in school. But he had faith that he could do better. Just because he had made one mistake didn't mean he was a failure. During the time he had left in college, he worked very hard. He graduated second in his class. His grades were now good enough for graduate school.

Throughout his life General Powell has remembered that lesson. "Everybody makes mistakes. We have to look at them and learn from them. But we can't dwell on them."

General Powell doesn't give up when he makes a mistake. He has faith in himself that with hard work and determination, he will do the right job the next time.

Even though Mark Wellman can't walk, he and his partner, Mike Corbett, climbed a 7,569-foot mountain in California.

5

WHAT IF YOU FAIL?

NOTHING VENTURED, NOTHING GAINED. Remember that old saying? Its message is simple. If you never *try* to reach a goal, you can be sure you never *will* reach it. But if you try, at least you've given yourself a chance.

Don't Be Afraid to Fail

Most people don't try because they are afraid of failing. Mark Wellman failed when he tried to climb Gables Peak in Yosemite National Park. He fell 50 feet and was paralyzed from the waist down. Doctors told him he would never walk again. But he was determined to keep climbing. Failure wasn't going to stop him.

Seven years after his fall, Mark went back to Yosemite. This time he tried El Capitan, one of the toughest rock climbs in America. He was still paralyzed. He could not use his legs. But he was very determined. It took Mark 7

43

Chapter Five

days and 4 hours to climb the 3,200-foot peak. He pulled himself up slowly with his arms, 6 inches at a time, 7,000 times. He succeeded because he tried again.

Says Mark, "My whole thing in life is finding another way to do it." He found another way to climb the peak without using his legs. If he had quit after his first failure, he never would have succeeded.

Don't Quit When You Get Discouraged

Your failure may happen slowly over a long time. You just seem to be going nowhere. This slow kind of failure can make you very discouraged.

Rita Moreno, the famous actress, knew all about slow failure. Rita was born in Puerto Rico. Her parents divorced, and she came to New York with her mother. They lived in a run-down apartment. The future looked dark.

Rita's only bright spot was her dancing lessons. She did so well that she was offered parts in children's plays. Soon she had a small part in a Broadway play. After many tries she broke into the movies. But in each one Rita played the same kind of person. She was always a wild and sexy Latin lady, and she didn't like it.

Rita became very discouraged. Her career was going nowhere. Still, she didn't quit. After what seemed like a long time without success, *Life* magazine did a story on her. That story led to some new movies, playing parts she liked better.

Today Rita Moreno is listed in the *Guinness Book of World Records*. She has won the four biggest United States entertainment awards: an Oscar, a Tony, a Grammy, and two Emmys. Rita did not let failure get her down. Instead, her failures made her even more determined to get to the top.

Have you ever been scared of failure? Maybe it's happened in school. Your history grades have been going down all year. Now it's time for the last test. Unless you do very well, you won't pass the course. You're scared. What do you do? Do you panic? Do you become so afraid of failing that that's all you think about? Remember, you make more mistakes when you're running scared. The president of the United States during World War II, Franklin Roosevelt, once said, "We have nothing to fear but fear itself."

Always Be Willing to Start Over

If you get discouraged you may say, "Forget it. What's the point of studying? I haven't been able to do well all year. Nothing's going to change now."

46
Chapter Five

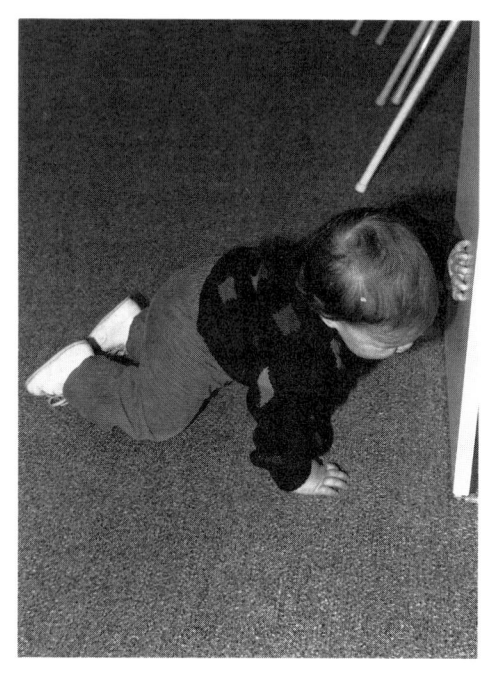

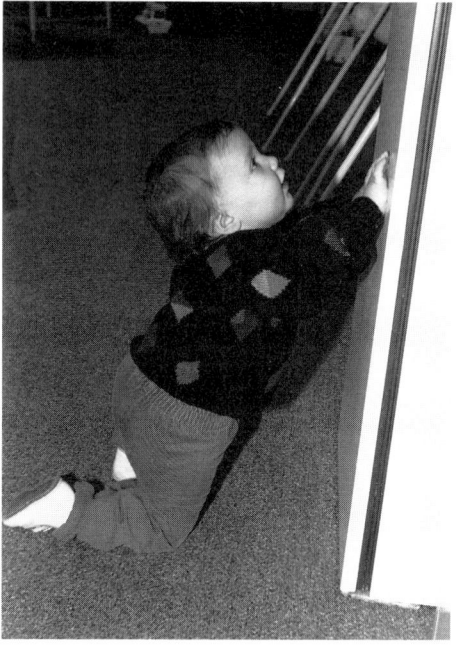

But if you get tough with yourself, you say, "YES! I'm going to turn in a test that will make that teacher fall back in his chair. He doesn't think I can do it, but I know I can." It's late in the year, but you can start over.

Failing is a big part of learning. You weren't born knowing how to talk or write your name. You had to try, practice, and fail many times before you learned. The same is true of any goal.

Milton Hershey was a man who kept trying. As a boy, his family moved a lot. He went to seven schools in eight years. Finally, in the fourth grade Milton quit. He went

47
What If You Fail?

Children learn the value of determination at an early age, when almost everything in life is a new challenge.

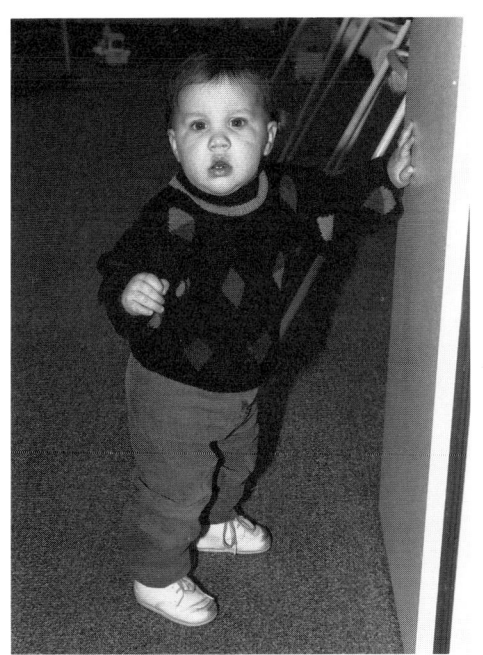

to work for a printer. He was fired. Next he worked for a candy maker. Soon he started his own business. It failed. He moved to Denver and tried again. That business failed. On to New York for one more try. Again the business failed. But through all those failures Milton had been learning.

Finally he returned to Pennsylvania. There he found something that worked—making caramels. At age 36 he began making chocolate. After many failures he was at last on his way to success. Milton Hershey (as you may have guessed) was the man behind Hershey's chocolate.

Chapter Five

Learn to Live with Criticism

The road to success is not often lined with people cheering you along. Authors know this. Most of them get dozens of rejection letters before their first book is ever published. Even when it is, reviewers may say bad things about it in the papers.

Criticism hurts. Some criticism is unfair. But a determined person will not be discouraged by it. He or she will forget what is unfair and learn from the constructive criticism.

John Johnson had a goal. He wanted to start a magazine. But he needed $500. That was a lot of money for a poor boy from Arkansas to raise in 1942. When he went to a bank the banker laughed at him. "We don't make loans to colored people," he said.

Sure it was unfair. But Johnson remembered the books he'd been reading about helping yourself. They said, "Don't get mad, get smart." So Johnson got smart. "If you won't lend me the money, then who in this town will?" he asked the banker. The surprised banker suggested a company. Johnson asked for the name of the person he should see. "May I tell him you referred me?" Johnson asked. Still more surprised, the banker agreed.

John Johnson was on his way. He had not let criticism stop him. There were many other obstacles on the road to his goal. But he never got discouraged. "At every turning point in my life, people told me 'no' at first. But I refused to give up."

Today John Johnson is the president of the Johnson Publishing Company. His first magazine was *Negro Digest*. Now the company publishes *Ebony* and *Jet* and also owns TV and radio stations. Johnson has written a book called *Succeeding Against the Odds*.

What If You Try Hard and Still Fail?

"All you can do is all you can do. . . ." This is the motto of Art Williams. He is the man who started one of the biggest money management businesses in America. Says Williams, "Sometimes no matter what you do, no matter how hard you try, things don't turn out the way you've planned. . . . This is the time when a lot of people want to quit. They feel like they've failed because they just couldn't turn events around."

Failure happens to all of us. When it does, says Williams, "There's only one thing left to do. You need to accept the situation. Accept the fact that you've taken a wrong turn."

There's a second part to Williams' saying: "But all you can do is enough. When you've truly made your best

Chapter Five

In November, 1990, Bill Irwin became the first blind man to hike the 2,000-mile Appalachian Trail.

effort, you've done enough. You've done everything anyone could do. And that's all that anyone expects of you. It's all you can expect of yourself."

But then what? Do you quit? Do you give up your goal? Then, Williams says, "You've got to start moving forward again. It may mean changing directions. It may mean working toward your goals from another angle. What you can't do is worry yourself crazy about it or let it defeat you. If you do, you will destroy your determination to succeed."

You can test your outlook on life by deciding if this glass is half full or half empty.

6

THE IMPORTANCE OF BEING POSITIVE

HALF THE CUP HAS WATER IN IT. Is it half full or half empty? If you say half full, you're thinking positively. (At least part of it is filled and that's a good start!) If you say it's half empty, you're thinking negatively. (Look, half the water is already gone and I'll probably spill the rest!)

There is more to this message than half a cup of water. The message is about your attitude, the way you look at an idea. Think negatively and you'll get negative results. Think positively and you'll get positive results. It's nearly that simple! Dr. Norman Vincent Peale, the famous minister, is the father of the "Positive Thinking" movement. He wrote a book called *The Power of Positive Thinking*. In it he talks about believing in yourself.

Dr. Peale had a chance to try out positive thinking in his own life. He wanted to start a new magazine. But soon after it began, he ran out of money. Most of the people working with him were ready to quit.

Chapter Six

But one worker had a different attitude. Instead of being discouraged because the magazine had few readers, she was thankful for those they did have. She was thankful for new ideas that made the magazine better. Her positive attitude spread to the others. Soon they began to have faith in themselves again. They gave the magazine one more chance. Today, *Guideposts* is one of the most widely read magazines in the world.

Success Doesn't Come to Those Who Doubt

Althea Gibson was born in South Carolina in 1927. Back then, a black girl had little chance of making something of herself. While she was still a child, her family moved to a poor part of New York City. Her chances there were no better. But Althea never doubted she would make it.

"I was determined to be something if it killed me." Sports was one of the few avenues for success open to black people during that time. Althea met a rich doctor who lived in North Carolina. He paid for her tennis lessons. Blacks were not allowed on public tennis courts. But she practiced hard in the doctor's backyard. Soon she was playing in the ATA, the black American tennis circuit.

Althea didn't complain when people treated her unfairly because she was black. Instead she practiced. She worked hard and stayed positive. She believed in herself.

The Importance of Being Positive

And she never gave up her goal of becoming somebody.

Althea Gibson's positive thinking paid off. She played at Wimbledon, England, in one of the biggest tennis matches in the world. She won. In America she won the U.S. Nationals. She met the Queen of England and got a letter from the president of the United States. Thanks to her determination, Althea Gibson did become somebody.

Slap Yourself on the Wrist, but Pat Yourself on the Back

Even with all the determination in the world, you'll still make mistakes. Everyone does. The secret to positive thinking is how you handle those mistakes. Do you see each one as a big failure? Or do you see it as a good lesson that can help you toward your goal? Look at your mistakes only long enough to learn from them. Slap yourself on the wrist and say, "That was a bad idea. But what can I learn from it?" Then move forward.

Determination will also bring successes. How will you handle those? Will you sneer at yourself and say, "Well it's about time. I hope I'm not dead before the next good thing happens." Or will you pat yourself on the back and say, "I've done all right! I'm going to tell someone about this." Being positive will give you a good feeling about yourself. Positive thinking means knowing how to handle your successes as well as your mistakes.

Chapter Six

Set Your Standards High

You get out of life what you expect from it. If you expect to fail, you probably will. If you expect to do OK, you'll probably lead an OK life. But if you expect great things of yourself, you'll come out on top. What it takes is determination. Faith in yourself that you can and you will. A positive attitude.

Today we remember Abraham Lincoln as one of the greatest American presidents—maybe *the* greatest. Why was Lincoln great? Because he believed he could be great.

It wasn't easy. His family was very poor. School was two miles away, through the woods. It was a long walk for a small boy. When Abe was only nine his mother died. He went to work for a farmer to help his family. Then there was no time for school.

But Abraham Lincoln was determined to be great. He set high standards for himself. Getting an education was his first goal. At night Lincoln would read by the light of a small fire. He studied hard to become a lawyer.

All through his life, Lincoln faced one obstacle after another. He lost his first election to the Senate. Three of his children died. Even after he was elected president, the newspapers made fun of him. They called him "Honest Ape." They said it was a bad joke that someone with so little schooling could be president.

The Importance of Being Positive

Determination as a group can often be used to achieve positive results in a community.

Chapter Six

During the Civil War, Lincoln faced the biggest obstacle of all. The country was torn apart. People in the southern states wanted to own slaves. People in the northern states were against slavery. Lincoln tried very hard to keep his nation together. It was nearly an impossible job. Lincoln became very discouraged. People on both sides were very angry with him, but he did what he believed was right. He followed his own heart. Abraham Lincoln faced these obstacles with faith in himself and a determination to hold the country together.

Lincoln expected a lot from himself. He expected a lot from his country. He believed that he and America could be great. Lincoln led the country through some of the hardest and darkest times. But we did become a great nation, and Abraham Lincoln became one of our greatest leaders.

Never stop trying. You are not born being a determined person. You must work at it. Determination is something you build inside yourself by believing that you can and will reach a goal.

Calvin Coolidge, another U.S. president, said this about determination: "Nothing in this world can take the place of persistence. Talent will not. . . Genius will not. . . Education will not. . . Persistence and determination alone are the powerful forces."

Glossary: *Explaining New Words*

attitude Outlook; a way of thinking, feeling, or acting.
belief An opinion or idea that a person feels is true or right.
commitment A pledge; a promise to work toward a goal.
criticism An opinion on whether an idea or action is good or bad. Often criticism is negative.
determination Deciding firmly to reach a goal.
genius A person who is very smart or has great ability and talent.
goal An aim or purpose. Something a person wants to accomplish.
hurdle A difficulty or problem that must be overcome.
immigrant A person who moves to a country other than that of his or her birth.
inspiration An idea or action that causes a person to

Glossary

think, feel, or act in a certain way.

motto A short saying that tells what a person believes in or stands for.

obstacle A hurdle. Something that stands in the way of progress.

panic Fear so strong that it causes a person to lose control and want to run.

paralyzed Unable to move a part of the body.

patience The ability to put up with failure, problems, or delays without getting upset.

persistence The quality of not giving up; the ability to keep trying.

sacrifice To give up something of value for the sake of something else.

self-discipline Training or being strict with oneself.

standards Guidelines; principles; rules or qualities to judge by.

succeed To do well; to reach a goal.

venture To try to do something that has risk or danger.

For Further Reading

Carnegie, Dale, & Carnegie, Dorothy. *How to Win Friends and Influence People.* New York: Simon & Schuster, rev. ed. 1981. Tips on how to help you get along better with other people. Another good book by Dale Carnegie is *How to Stop Worrying and Start Living,* Simon & Schuster, rev. ed. 1984.

Elliott, Alan C. *A Daily Dose of the American Dream.* Dallas, TX: Saybrook Publishing, 1988. Stories behind some of America's most determined people—those who have built successful businesses. One story for every day of the year, from Famous Amos to Oprah Winfrey.

Guideposts Magazine. New York, NY. A monthly magazine that prints real- life stories about determination, success, positive attitudes, and reaching your goals.

Johnson, Ann D. *The Value of Determination: The Story of Helen Keller.* San Diego, CA: Value Communications, 1976. One of a series of stories with pictures about

For Further Reading

famous people whose values have helped them succeed. Other books from Value Communications: *The Value of Courage: The Story of Jackie Robinson; The Value of Facing a Challenge: The Story of Terry Fox; The Value of Believing in Yourself: The Story of Louis Pasteur; The Value of Patience: The Story of the Wright Brothers*

Johnson, John. *Succeeding Against the Odds.* New York: Warner Books, 1988. The story behind the founder of *Ebony* magazine.

Peale, Norman V. *The Power of Positive Thinking.* New York: Walker & Co., 1985. Building a positive attitude by changing your outlook. Another good book by Norman Vincent Peale is *You Can If You Think You Can.* Englewood Cliffs, NJ: Prentice-Hall, 1982.

Williams, Art. *All You Can Do Is All You Can Do, But All You Can Do Is Enough.* New York: Ballantine Books, 1988. A step-by-step plan to reaching your goals. Another good book by Art Williams is *Pushing Up People.* Doraville, GA: Parlake Publishers, 1984.

INDEX

A
Amos, Wally, 36
Attitude, 53

B
Beliefs, 8, 30-31, 33
Black Americans, 18
Braille, 15-16

C
Chekov family, 22, 24
Civil War, 58
Columbus, Christopher, 9-10
Commitment, 12
Communism, 12
Coolidge, Calvin, 58
Courage, 8
Criticism, 48

D
Determination, 7

E
Ebony magazine, 49
Edison, Thomas, 33
Ellis Island, 22, 24

F
Failure, 43-51
Faith, 8, 13, 19, 56, 58
Famous Amos cookies, 36

G
Germany, 18
Gibson, Althea, 54-55
Goals, 7, 19, 35-36, 39-40
Grand Canyon, 21-22
Guideposts magazine, 54
Guinness Book of World Records, 45

H
Hershey, Milton, 46-47
Hitler, Adolf, 18

I
Immigrants, 22
Indians, American, 18

J
Jet magazine, 49
Jews, 18
Johnson, John, 48-49
Jordan, Michael, 33

K
Keller, Helen, 15-16

L
L'Amour, Louis, 25
Learning, 46
Life magazine, 45
Lincoln, Abraham, 56, 58

M
Mayflower, 28, 30
Mistakes, 55
Mitchell, W., 37, 39
Moreno, Rita, 44-45

N
Negative thinking, 53
Negro Digest, 49
North Pole, 27-28
North to the Rails, 25

O
Obstacles, 16-25

Index

P
Pasteur, Louis, 19, 21
Patience, 8
Peale, Norman Vincent, 53
Peary, Robert E., 27-28
Persistence, 8, 9
Pilgrims, 28, 30
Positive thinking, 53
Powell, Colin, 40-41
Powell, John Wesley, 21-22
Power of Positive Thinking, The, 53
Pride, 36

R
Race, 18
Religion, 18
Rodriguez-Ybarra, Blanca, 7-8
Roosevelt, Franklin, 45

S
Sabin, Florence, 16, 18
Sacrifices, 39
Schoolwork, 45
Self-discipline, 16
Slavery, 58
Solidarity Movement, 12
Standards, 56
Succeeding Against the Odds, 49
Success, 33, 55
Sullivan, Anne, 15-16
Sun-Hak, Baik, 9

T
Tucker, Preston, 10

U
University of North Carolina, 33

V
Volunteer, 36

W
Walesa, Lech, 12
Washington, Yolanda, 31, 33
Waterford, 18-19
Wellman, Mark, 43-44
Williams, Art, 49, 51

Y
Yosemite National Park, 43-44

About the Author
Eleanor Ayer is the author of several books for young children and young adults. She has written about the Hispanic and Indian cultures, the natural history of the American West, and the recent unification of Germany. Eleanor holds a master's degree from Syracuse University with a specialty in literacy journalism.

Photo Credits and Acknowlegments
Cover Photo: Barbara Kirk
Photos on pages 2, 11, 14, 29, 41, 42, 50: Wide World; page 6, 17, 23, 26, 32, 34, 38, 57: Mary Lauzon; page 20, 46–47, 52: Stuart Rabinowitz

Design and Production: Blackbirch Graphics, Inc.

Robinson Township Public
Library District
606 N. Jefferson Street
Robinson, IL 62454